S0-AAH-140

2.0

DISCARDED

Shh, Can You Hear?

By JONATHAN PEALE

Illustrated by TOM HEARD

Music Produced by ERIK KOSKINEN and
Recorded at REAL PHONIC STUDIOS

CANTATA
LEARNING

WWW.CANTATALEARNING.COM

CANTATA LEARNING

Published by Cantata Learning
1710 Roe Crest Drive
North Mankato, MN 56003
www.cantatalearning.com

Copyright © 2017 Cantata Learning

All rights reserved. No part of this publication may be reproduced
in any form without written permission from the publisher.

A note to educators and librarians from the publisher: Cantata Learning has provided the following data to assist in book processing and suggested use of Cantata Learning product.

Publisher's Cataloging-in-Publication Data
Prepared by Librarian Consultant: Ann-Marie Begnaud
Library of Congress Control Number: 2015958195
      Shh, Can You Hear?
      Series: School Time Songs
      By Jonathan Peale
      Illustrated by Tom Heard
      Summary: A song that teaches students how to listen.
      ISBN: 978-1-63290-628-1 (library binding/CD)
      ISBN: 978-1-63290-648-9 (paperback/CD)
Suggested Dewey and Subject Headings:
      Dewey: E 395.5
      LCSH Subject Headings: Courtesy – Juvenile literature. | Students – Juvenile literature. | Courtesy – Songs and music -- Texts. | Students – Songs and music -- Texts. | Courtesy – Juvenile sound recordings. | Students – Juvenile sound recordings.
      Sears Subject Headings: Helping behavior. | Courtesy. | Students. | School songbooks. | Children's songs. | Folk music.
      BISAC Subject Headings: JUVENILE NONFICTION / School & Education. | JUVENILE NONFICTION / Music / Songbooks. | JUVENILE NONFICTION / Social Topics / Manners & Etiquette.

Book design and art direction, Tim Palin Creative
Editorial direction, Flat Sole Studio
Music direction, Elizabeth Draper
Music produced by Erik Koskinen and recorded at Real Phonic Studios

Printed in the United States of America in North Mankato, Minnesota.
072016   0335CGF16

ACCESS THE MUSIC!

SCAN CODE WITH MOBILE APP

CANTATALEARNING.COM

Animals listen to learn about the world around them. You can, too. Sit quietly like a mouse . . . a bear . . . or a cat. What do you hear? Listening helps you learn in school and shows that you respect others.

Turn the page to sing a song about listening with your classmates!

5

Shhh.

Let's listen.

Shhh.

Let's be still.

Can you hear something?

I'm sure that you will
if you're quiet as a mouse . . . or a bear . . . or a cat.

Shhh.
What's that?

Can you listen like a mouse
in your tiny little house?

Can you hear a piece of cheese?
Can you hear somebody sneeze?

You can hear somebody sigh.
You can hear a buzzing fly.

You can hear a cat go by,
if you listen
like a mouse!

Shhh.
Let's listen.

Shhh.
Let's be still.

Can you hear something?

I'm sure that you will
if you're quiet as a mouse . . . or a bear . . . or a cat.

Shhh.
What's that?

Can you listen like a cat?

Can your paws go pitter-pat?

Can your ears move fast and quick?

Can you hear the clock go "tick"?

You can hear the smallest sound,
something tiny on the ground.

Something tiny can be found,
if you listen
like a cat!

Shhh.
Let's listen.

Shhh.
Let's be still.

Can you hear something?

I'm sure that you will
if you're quiet as a mouse . . . or a bear . . . or a cat.

Shhh.
What's that?

Can you listen like a bear?

Can you hear things everywhere?

Put your paw to your ear.

It will help you hear.

You can hear outside the wall,
people talking in the hall,
if you make no sound at all,
if you listen
like a bear!

Hey, now, will you look at that?
You can listen like a cat,
like a mouse, and like a bear.

You can listen anywhere!

You can listen when you play.
You can hear a song today.

You can hear what others say
if you listen
just like you!

Shhh.

Let's listen.

Shhh.

Let's be still.

Can you hear something?

I'm sure that you will
if you're quiet as a mouse . . . or a bear . . . or a cat.

Shhh.

What's that?

Shhh,

What's that?

Shhh!

SONG LYRICS
Shh, Can You Hear?

Shhh.
Let's listen.
Shhh.
Let's be still.
Can you hear something?

I'm sure that you will
if you're quiet as a mouse . . .
  or a bear . . . or a cat.
Shhh.
What's that?

Can you listen like a mouse
in your tiny little house?
Can you hear a piece of cheese?
Can you hear somebody sneeze?

You can hear somebody sigh.
You can hear a buzzing fly.
You can hear a cat go by,
if you listen
like a mouse!

Shhh.
Let's listen.
Shhh.
Let's be still.
Can you hear something?

I'm sure that you will
if you're quiet as a mouse . . .
  or a bear . . . or a cat.
Shhh.
What's that?

Can you listen like a cat?
Can your paws go pitter-pat?
Can your ears move fast and quick?
Can you hear the clock go "tick"?

You can hear the smallest sound,
something tiny on the ground.
Something tiny can be found,
if you listen
like a cat!

Shhh.
Let's listen.
Shhh.
Let's be still.
Can you hear something?

I'm sure that you will
if you're quiet as a mouse . . .
  or a bear . . . or a cat.
Shhh.
What's that?

Can you listen like a bear?
Can you hear things everywhere?
Put your paw to your ear.
It will help you hear.

You can hear outside the wall,
people talking in the hall,
if you make no sound at all,
if you listen
like a bear!

Hey, now, will you look at that?
You can listen like a cat,
like a mouse, and like a bear.
You can listen anywhere!

You can listen when you play.
You can hear a song today.
You can hear what others say
if you listen
just like you!

Shhh.
Let's listen.
Shhh.
Let's be still.
Can you hear something?

I'm sure that you will
if you're quiet as a mouse . . .
  or a bear . . . or a cat.
Shhh.
What's that?

Shhh.
What's that?

Shhh!

Shh, Can You Hear?

Americana
Erik Koskinen

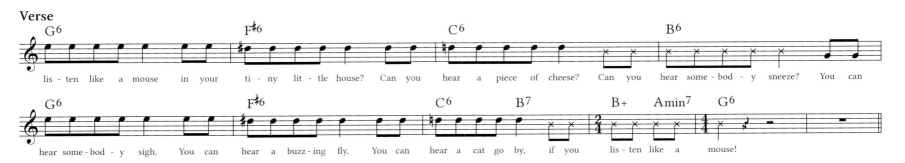

Chorus

Verse 2
Can you listen like a cat?
Can your paws go pitter-pat?
Can your ears move fast and quick?
Can you hear the clock go "tick"?

You can hear the smallest sound,
something tiny on the ground.
Something tiny can be found,
if you listen like a cat!

Chorus

Verse 3
Can you listen like a bear?
Can you hear things everywhere?
Put your paw to your ear.
It will help you hear.

You can hear outside the wall,
people talking in the hall,
if you make no sound at all,
if you listen like a bear!

Verse 4
Hey, now, will you look at that?
You can listen like a cat,
like a mouse, and like a bear.
You can listen anywhere!

You can listen when you play.
You can hear a song today.
You can hear what others say
if you listen just like you!

Chorus

GUIDED READING ACTIVITIES

1. Think about your day. What kinds of sounds do you listen for? What sounds do you like to hear? What sounds do you not like to hear?

2. Why is it important to listen at school? What could happen if you don't listen?

3. Go outside with an adult. Close your eyes and listen carefully. Tell the adult about all the sounds you hear. If you don't know what a sound is, you can ask the adult to help you.

TO LEARN MORE

Dahl, Michael. *Little Elephant Listens*. Minneapolis, MN: Picture Window Books, 2014.

Jones, Christianne C. *Lacey Walker, Nonstop Talker*. Minneapolis, MN: Picture Window Books, 2012.

Laffin, Jenna. *How Do We Listen?* Mankato, MN: Cantata Learning, 2016.

Nelson, Maria. *I Can Listen*. New York: Gareth Stevens, 2013.